HOW CAN I HAVE PEACE IN
LIFE'S STORMS?

✘ CULTIVATING BIBLICAL GODLINESS

Series Editors
Joel R. Beeke and Ryan M. McGraw

Dr. D. Martyn Lloyd-Jones once said that what the church needs to do most of all is "to begin herself to live the Christian life. If she did that, men and women would be crowding into our buildings. They would say, 'What is the secret of this?'" As Christians, one of our greatest needs is for the Spirit of God to cultivate biblical godliness in us in order to put the beauty of Christ on display through us, all to the glory of the triune God. With this goal in mind, this series of booklets treats matters vital to Christian experience at a basic level. Each booklet addresses a specific question in order to inform the mind, warm the affections, and transform the whole person by the Spirit's grace, so that the church may adorn the doctrine of God our Savior in all things.

HOW CAN I HAVE PEACE IN
LIFE'S STORMS?

BRIAN VOS

REFORMATION HERITAGE BOOKS
GRAND RAPIDS, MICHIGAN

How Can I Have Peace in Life's Storms?
© 2019 by Brian Vos

All rights reserved. No part of this book may be used or reproduced in any manner whatsoever without written permission except in the case of brief quotations embodied in critical articles and reviews. Direct your requests to the publisher at the following address:

Reformation Heritage Books
2965 Leonard St. NE
Grand Rapids, MI 49525
616-977-0889
orders@heritagebooks.org
www.heritagebooks.org

Printed in the United States of America
19 20 21 22 23 24/10 9 8 7 6 5 4 3 2 1

ISBN 978-1-60178-700-2
ISBN 978-1-60178-701-9 (e-pub)

For additional Reformed literature, request a free book list from Reformation Heritage Books at the above regular or e-mail address.

HOW CAN I HAVE PEACE IN
LIFE'S STORMS?

It was one of the most terrifying nights of my life. Thunder rumbled powerfully in the skies, shaking the earth beneath. Lightning flashed relentlessly in the dark, illumining the night sky. As the wind howled viciously, branches were torn from the trees around us. Rain pelted on the roof of our threatened feeble quarters. My wife and I huddled together with our little children on one end of our pop-up trailer, unable to sleep, fearing for our lives. It didn't help that only a few camping trips earlier we had witnessed a massive tree come down in the midst of a storm, slicing through a hard-sided trailer like a knife through warm butter, narrowly missing those inside. Here we were, not in a hard-sided trailer but in a canvas pop-up trailer in the middle of a storm that raged stronger and longer than any I had ever experienced before.

Earlier that evening we had moved all the sleeping bags to one end of the trailer, reassured our children, prayed with them, and then tried to sleep.

My prayers continued fervently for our safety. After three or four hours of sleeplessness, peppered with many prayers and recitations of Scripture, with the storm raging as fierce as ever, peace and stillness were given to me. My life, as well as the lives of my wife and children, were in the Lord's hands (Ps. 31:14–15), and there is none like Him, a God who rides the heavens to help, through the skies in His majesty. The eternal God is our dwelling place, and underneath are the everlasting arms (Deut. 33:26–27). The Lord is our keeper (Ps. 121:5).

Nearly everyone has experienced threatening storms of one kind or another that have filled their hearts with fear. Storms provide an apt metaphor for life. The storms of life batter every one of us. No one is exempt. These storms may differ in degree and duration, but they do come for all. You can look back and identify the storms of your life. Most likely you are able to pick out one or two storms that were extraordinarily difficult: the death of a loved one, cancer, illness, divorce, a wayward child, a friendship broken, a relationship destroyed, job loss, financial crisis, a church split, or a spiritual crisis. Perhaps you are in the middle of a storm now, and that is why you are reading this booklet. Life at present seems loud and blinding; the storm is driving you all about, threatening to consume you. You are afraid, and you don't know how you will weather this storm—or if you will. Fear has taken hold of you and peace is gone. Or perhaps your life is calm now, but you are fearful of the storms that may come: What if my spouse dies? What if I get cancer? What if my children stray? What if I lose my job? What if I am robbed? What if I am assaulted? What if I give in to temptation? What if I fall into grievous sin? What if I stray from the Lord? What if I lose my way? Storms have come in the past, or they may be raging in the present. Storms will come in the future. How can I have peace in life's storms?

God has given us His Word to serve as a lamp to our feet and a light to our path (Ps. 119:105). In God's Word we find a story of Jesus's disciples caught on the sea in the dark in a terrible storm. John records the scene:

> And when even was now come, his disciples went down unto the sea, and entered into a ship, and went over the sea toward Capernaum. And it was now dark, and Jesus was not come to them. And the sea arose by reason of a great wind that blew. So when they had rowed about five and twenty or thirty furlongs, they see Jesus walking on the sea, and drawing nigh unto the ship: and they were afraid. But he saith unto them, It is I; be not afraid. Then they willingly received him into the ship: and immediately the ship was at the land whither they went. (John 6:16–21)

This passage gives us five useful instructions for cultivating peace in life's storms: (1) recognize that the darkness will come; (2) believe that Jesus is on our side; (3) listen to the word; (4) reflect on the character of God; and (5) look to the joy that comes in the morning.

RECOGNIZE THAT THE DARKNESS WILL COME

It had been a remarkable day with Jesus. With five barley loaves and two fish, Jesus had miraculously fed thousands, so that all had their fill. There was even an abundance left over. So amazed were the people that they confessed Jesus to be the Prophet who is to come into the world (John 6:14). They wanted to take Jesus by force to make Him king, but He withdrew to the mountain by Himself (vv. 1–15). But the day was far spent and evening had come (v. 16). Darkness was overcoming the light. Nevertheless, the disciples, many of them trained fishermen, went down to the sea, got into a boat, and started across. By the time they were some distance out, it was dark, and Jesus had not yet come to them (v. 17).

The disciples did not follow Jesus up the mountain. Instead, they went down to the deep. They were now in the dark, alone and without Jesus. Darkness had fallen, and the One who brings light and life was not there. John records the scene in great detail, with pictures that are reminiscent of creation. Darkness is over the face of the deep. The scene sounds very much like Genesis 1:2, where the earth was void and without form. In that scene the Spirit was hovering over the face of the waters to bring light and life, but in this scene Jesus is not with them. They are separated from Him. How very dark it is.

The darkness did not strike fear in the hearts of the disciples, however. They were fishermen by trade. They had fished these waters many times and were familiar with the sea. The Sea of Galilee is six hundred feet below sea level, situated between two mountain ranges, which make it a wind tunnel of sorts. These fishermen knew that storms could rise up suddenly on the Sea of Galilee, and on this night, one did. The sea became rough because a strong wind was blowing (John 6:18). It was not the Spirit hovering over the face of the waters to bring light and life as it was in Genesis 1:2; it was the wind blowing over the face of the waters threatening to destroy life in the darkness in John 6. Nevertheless, the disciples kept rowing. They knew the darkness would come; they knew that storms could come. They had no fear of the darkness or even of the storms, despite Jesus not being with them.

What accounts for their fearlessness in the dark—their bravery in the storm? Certainly if Jesus were there, they would not be afraid. But Jesus is not there. He is still on the mountain. How then is their peace in the storm to be explained? In Matthew's account of this episode, we learn that Jesus made the disciples get into the boat and go before Him to the other side while He dismissed the crowds. After He had dismissed them, He went up on the mountain by Himself to pray (Matt. 14:22–23). Herein lies the explanation for the disciples' fearlessness in the dark on the face of the deep and the reason for their peace in the midst of the storm. Though Jesus was not physically present with them, He was praying for them.[1] His prayers sustained them in the darkness on the face of the deep. His intercession gave them peace in the midst of the storm.

There is peace here for believers. The darkness and storms of life will come. There is heartache in every pew and brokenness in every life. Though the darkness may hide Jesus's face and the storms may lead you to wonder whether He is with you, by faith you may stand on the firm foundation of His Word. In that Word He tells you that He is interceding for you (Rom. 8:34). He always lives to make intercession for you (Heb. 7:25). How precious are His prayers for you when the darkness comes! How comforting to know that He is praying for you in life's storms! He takes your name on His lips before the throne of your Father in heaven. He carries you on His heart in the presence of your Father's throne. He knows you better than you could ever know yourself. He understands your circumstances better than you could ever understand them yourself. He knows the end from the beginning. By His prayers

---

1. William Hendriksen, *Matthew* (1973; repr., Grand Rapids: Baker, 2004), 599. Hendriksen writes, "We are on safe ground…in maintaining that in the quiet of the evening indicated here in Matt. 14:23 Jesus, in solitary communion with his Father, prayed not for himself alone, but also for his disciples."

He upholds you, especially in the dark times of life, in the storms. Where do you turn when all around you is darkness and when the storms of life encompass you? Where do you find peace in the hardest times of life? Turn to the Word of God. Look to your heavenly Intercessor and find peace in His perfect prayers. The darkness will come, but Jesus is praying and interceding for you.

BELIEVE THAT JESUS IS ON OUR SIDE

After rowing three or four miles, the disciples saw Jesus walking on the sea and coming near the boat (John 6:19). The sea was rough. The waters were roaring and troubled, yet Jesus was walking on the waters, as though He had taken the place of the Spirit from Genesis 1:2. The only question was whether He was coming to bring light and life, like the Spirit did in creation, or to destroy life in the darkness, undoing creation in judgment. The disciples were fearful of the latter. It is striking that John says nothing of the disciples' fearing the darkness on the deep in the storm. But once they saw Jesus coming to them, their fears arose. No doubt remembering the scene vividly, John simply writes, "They were afraid" (v. 19). He remembers the storm, but even more than that he remembers Jesus walking on the water toward them and the fear that took hold of them all. The coming of Jesus in the storm brought them no peace.

Why were the disciples frightened when they saw Jesus? Perhaps they were frightened because they had failed Him so miserably that day. It had been a remarkable day, but also a day that exposed the weakness of their faith. They had failed the test Jesus had set before them when He asked Philip where they could buy bread to feed the large crowd:

> Philip answered him, Two hundred pennyworth of bread is not sufficient for them, that every one of them may take a little. One of his disciples, Andrew, Simon Peter's brother, saith unto him, There is a lad here, which hath five barley loaves, and two small fishes: but what are they among so many? (John 6:5–9)

Both Philip and Andrew had failed the test, as did the rest of the disciples, for none of them said anything. By their answers Philip and Andrew had implied that while Jesus was willing to feed the multitudes, He lacked the ability to do so. Their faith in Jesus was weak. As they saw Jesus approaching the boat with darkness all around and in the midst of a storm, perhaps they were afraid that He was angry with them. Perhaps they feared that He was going to rebuke them or even destroy them in this storm as a judgment on them for their lack of faith, their doubts, their sins. Here it becomes clear that John's reference to the darkness is not only to the time of day, but to the threat of spiritual darkness. The disciples' failures and sins have led them to doubt the character of God.

So often that is the way it seems with the storms of life. We live in a fallen, dark world that is no friend to grace. We know that the storms of life will come just as certainly as the darkness of night closes out every day. But sometimes, when life's storms come, we can convince ourselves that these storms are God's judgment on us for our sins. Maybe my loved one died because of my sin. Maybe I have cancer because God is against me. Maybe I lost my job because God is no longer on my side. So quickly we adopt the theology of Job's friends. If you are suffering the storms of life, you might think that God has something against you, that He is not on your side, that He is coming to you in judgment for your sin, that there is still wrath for you to bear. Such a view only increases the fear and terror of the storm because now behind a frowning providence lies the frown of an angry God and a just judge. How often we doubt God's goodness in the midst of life's storms. How often we think that He is coming to us as a just judge to punish us in wrath rather than as a merciful father to correct us in love.

While there are times when God disciplines us for our sin, He does not judge us for our sin. Christ has borne that judgment for us once and for all. There is therefore now no condemnation for those who are in Christ Jesus (Rom. 8:1). In Christ, you can be assured that He is not coming to you as a just judge to punish you in your sin but as a merciful father to correct you in love. He does not send storms into your life to drive you from Him. He sends them into your life to draw you to Him. His intent is not that you turn your face away in doubt and bitterness but that you turn your face toward Him in trust and faith. The author of Hebrews says,

> And ye have forgotten the exhortation which speaketh unto you as unto children, My son, despise not thou the chastening of the Lord, nor faint when thou are rebuked of him: for whom the Lord loveth He chasteneth, and scourgeth every son whom He receiveth. If ye endure chastening, God dealeth with you as with sons; for what son is he whom the father chasteneth not? But if ye be without chastisement, whereof all are partakers, then are ye bastards, and not sons. Furthermore, we have had fathers of our flesh which corrected us, and we gave them reverence: shall we not much rather be in subjection unto the Father of spirits, and live? For they verily for a few days chastened us after their own pleasure; but he for our profit, that we might be partakers of His holiness. Now no chastening for the present seemeth to be joyous, but grievous: nevertheless afterward it yieldeth the peaceable fruit of righteousness unto them which are exercised thereby. (Heb. 12:5–11)

Here the author of Hebrews makes clear that chastening and discipline is not only proof of your sonship but even more of the Father's love for you. The trials of life are not evidence that God is against you. They are the evidence that God is for you.

There is peace here for believers. God is not against His people. He is for His people. Even in the darkness, even in the storms, He comes to you not for your harm but for your good. He afflicts you not to destroy you but to restore you. Where do you turn when all around you is darkness and when the storms of life encompass you? Where do you find peace in the hardest times of life? Turn to the Word of God. Look to the One who is on your side, and find peace in His loving correction. The storms will come, but Jesus is on your side. He assures you that behind a frowning providence hides a smiling face—the face of your heavenly Father who loves you.

LISTEN TO THE WORD

Jesus did not come to the disciples to harm them, nor did He come to them because He was against them. On the contrary, He came to them to comfort them and because He was for them. He came to bring them His word.

The disciples were frightened when Jesus came to them, but as Jesus drew near the boat He spoke His word to them. The first words out of His mouth to His fearful disciples were these: "It is I; be not afraid" (John 6:20). In the original language, Jesus literally says, "I Am; do not fear." In Exodus 3, God revealed Himself to Moses at the burning bush and called him to bring His people out of Egypt, but Moses objected. In the course of his objections, Moses said to God,

> Behold, when I come unto the children of Israel, and shall say unto them, The God of your

> fathers hath sent me to you; and they shall say to me, What is His name? What shall I say unto them? And God said unto Moses, I AM THAT I AM: and he said, Thus shalt thou say unto the children of Israel, I AM hath sent me unto you. (Ex. 3:13–14)

As Jesus came to His disciples on the water, He took this name on His lips. He is the One who spoke to Moses at the burning bush and who now speaks to the disciples on the water. In Exodus 3, God revealed Himself to Moses as I Am at the burning bush, and the fire did not consume him. In John 6, Jesus reveals Himself to the disciples as I Am on the water, and the waters cannot overcome them.

Earlier in the day the crowds had confessed Jesus to be the Prophet; they had wanted to make Him a king. Here Jesus identifies Himself not simply as a prophet or king but as the great I Am. He made the waters and rules over them. They belong to Him. Of course He can walk on them! He walks on the waters here not to consume His fearful disciples but to save them. He is not against them. He is for them. Immediately after identifying Himself as I Am, Jesus speaks a good word to His disciples: "Do not be afraid." He knows their failures, doubts, sins, and fear. He does not come to them in spite of their failures, doubts, sins, and fears. He comes to them *because* of their failures, doubts, sins, and fears. He wants them to know He is with them in the darkness and on the deep. He is with them, the waters cannot overcome them. He is the refuge and strength of His people. He is a very present help in trouble:

> Therefore we will not fear, though the earth be removed, and though the mountains be carried into the midst of the sea; though the waters thereof roar and be troubled, though the mountains shake with the swelling thereof. There is a river, the streams whereof shall make glad the city of God, the holy place of the tabernacles of the most High. God is in the midst of her; she shall not be moved: God shall help her, and that right early. The heathen raged, the kingdoms were moved: he uttered his voice, the earth melted. The LORD of hosts is with us; the God of Jacob is our refuge. (Ps. 46:2–7)

As Jesus utters His voice, the King of creation speaks, and His word creates that of which it speaks. He says, "Do not be afraid," and immediately the disciples' fear is gone. Here is a word spoken into the darkness to bring light, life, gladness, and joy. That is what the Word of God does in our trials, in those dark times, life's storms. In those times when the waters threaten to overcome us, His Word serves as our firm foundation, as the hymn so beautifully professes:

> How firm a foundation, ye saints of the Lord,
> Is laid for your faith in His excellent Word!
> What more can He say than to you He has said,
> To you who for refuge to Jesus have fled?

> When through the deep waters I call thee to go,
> The rivers of sorrow shall not overflow;
> For I will be with thee thy trials to bless,
> And sanctify to thee thy deepest distress.
>
> The soul that on Jesus has leaned for repose,
> I will not, I will not desert to his foes;
> That soul, though all hell should endeavor to shake,
> I'll never, no never, no never forsake![2]

There is peace here for believers. God has spoken His word to you and said, "I Am! Do not be afraid!" He speaks to you in His Word not to harm you but to help you. He gives you His Word not to destroy you but to save you. He speaks to you in His Word not to create storms in your life but to give you peace in the midst of them. He reveals Himself to you in His Word not to shut you out in darkness but to give you light in the darkest night. Where do you turn when all around you is darkness and the storms of life encompass you? Where do you find peace in the hardest times of life? Turn to the Word of God. Listen to the One who has revealed Himself to you in His Word. Find peace in His Word to you. The storms will come, but Jesus has given you His Word and assures you He is God, and you need not be afraid.

---

2. "How Firm a Foundation," in *Psalter Hymnal* (Grand Rapids: Board of Publications of the Christian Reformed Church, 1976), #411, vv. 1, 3, 5.

REFLECT ON THE CHARACTER OF GOD

When Jesus said to His fearful disciples, "I Am; do not be afraid," they were glad to take Him into the boat (John 6:21). The original language conveys more than gladness. They *desired* to take Him into the boat. They wanted His presence and to have fellowship and communion with Him. He was there not in judgment and wrath but in mercy to comfort and to cheer, so their fear was gone and was replaced with gladness. John does not tell us whether the wind and the waves were stilled. In John's recollection of that evening, it was not the calming of the wind and waves that mattered. It was the presence of Jesus that mattered. Jesus was not with the disciples to judge them for their failures and sins but to comfort them as the forgiver of their failures and sins. No wonder they received Him with gladness!

It was for this that Moses prayed after the people's tragic sin of making for themselves the golden calf at the foot of Sinai. The Lord descended in the cloud and stood with Moses and proclaimed the name of the Lord:

> The LORD, The LORD God, merciful and gracious, longsuffering, and abundant in goodness and truth, keeping mercy for thousands, forgiving iniquity and transgression and sin, and that will by no means clear the guilty; visiting the iniquity of the fathers upon the children, and upon the children's children, unto the third and to the fourth generation. (Ex. 34:6–7)

God reveals Himself first as a God of mercy and grace. Though He is also a God of justice, who will by no means clear the guilty, He has taken the guilt of His people to Himself in His Son to clear them. Even in wrath, God remembers mercy (Hab. 3:2).

Moses's response to God's self-revelation is most instructive: "And Moses made haste, and bowed his head toward the earth, and worshipped. And he said, If now I have found grace in thy sight, O LORD, let my LORD, I pray thee, go among us; for it is a stiffnecked people; and pardon our iniquity and our sin, and take us for thine inheritance" (Ex. 34:8–9). Moses worships God because of who He is and pleads for the presence of God because the people are stiff-necked and sinful. In other words, Moses wants God to go with them *because* He is a God of mercy and grace—a God who pardons iniquity and sin, taking redeemed sinners for His inheritance. The disciples respond in much the same way that night in the darkness on the face of the deep. With gladness they received Jesus into the boat because of who Jesus is—because He is kind and gracious, because He pardons and forgives, because He is the friend of sinners.

There is peace here for believers. When darkness surrounds you, when the waters threaten to overcome you, when life's storms assail you, you do well to reflect on the character of God. His character is revealed to you most fully in Jesus: "No man hath seen God at any time, the only begotten Son, which is in the bosom of the Father, he hath declared him"

(John 1:18). If you want to know what God is like, you have to look no further than Jesus. Jesus is the revelation of God because He is God (vv. 1–2). Your comfort, your hope, and your peace are found in Him:

> My hope is built on nothing less
> Than Jesus' blood and righteousness;
> I dare not trust the sweetest frame,
> But wholly lean on Jesus' name.
>
> When darkness veils His lovely face,
> I rest on his unchanging grace;
> In ev'ry high and stormy gale,
> My anchor holds within the veil.
>
> His oath, His covenant, His blood
> Support me in the 'whelming flood;
> When all around my soul gives way,
> He then is all my hope and stay.
>
> When he shall come with trumpet sound,
> O may I then in him be found.
> Dressed in His righteousness alone,
> Faultless to stand before the throne.
>
> On Christ, the solid rock, I stand;
> All other ground is sinking sand.[3]

Peace in life's storms is not found as much in your hold on God as it is in His hold on you. Your

---

[3]. Edward Mote, "My Hope Is Built on Nothing Less," in *Trinity Psalter Hymnal* (Willow Grove, Pa.: Trinity Psalter Joint Venture, 2018), #459.

hold on Him can grow weak. His hold on you never does. It is not your character that saves; it is His character that saves. Your commitment to Him wanes, but His commitment to you never does. Your love for Him grows cold. His love for you never does. Where do you turn when all around you is darkness and when the storms of life encompass you? Where do you find peace in the hardest times of life? Turn to the Word of God. Reflect on the character of God as He has revealed Himself in His Word. Find peace in who He is. He will not leave you nor forsake you (Heb. 13:5). As the author of Lamentations wrote in a time of great suffering, "This I recall to my mind, therefore have I hope. It is of the LORD's mercies that we are not consumed, because his compassions fail not. They are new every morning: great is thy faithfulness. The LORD is my portion, saith my soul; therefore will I hope in him (Lam. 3:21–24).

LOOK TO THE JOY THAT COMES IN THE MORNING

Jesus reveals His character still further after getting into the boat with His disciples. The disciples received Him into the boat with gladness, "and immediately the ship was at the land whither they went" (John 6:21). With Jesus they arrived safely on shore. The waters could not overwhelm them, nor could the storm touch them. The darkness could not consume them. Jesus was their safety, their security, their refuge, and their strength. He was their very present help in trouble, their ark in the midst of

Look to the Joy That Comes in the Morning 19

the storm. He was the one who carried them safely through the waters to dry land. As we remember the creation themes of this passage, John's point becomes clear: Jesus brings His people safely through the storm to the new creation.

John places the story here in his gospel for this reason. Nearly all of John 6 is focused on Jesus as the bread of life. Jesus feeds the thousands with bread in verses 1–15. He goes on to identify Himself as the bread of life in verses 22–71, revealing Himself as one greater than Moses: "Verily, verily, I say unto you, Moses gave you not that bread from heaven; but my Father giveth you the true bread from heaven. For the bread of God is he which cometh down from heaven, and giveth life unto the world" (vv. 32–33). He goes on to say,

> I am that bread of life. Your fathers did eat manna in the wilderness, and are dead. This is the bread which cometh down from heaven, that a man may eat thereof, and not die. I am the living bread which came down from heaven: if any man eat of this bread, he shall live for ever: and the bread that I will give is my flesh, which I will give for the life of the world. (vv. 48–51)

He then declares still further:

> Verily, verily, I say unto you, Except ye eat the flesh of the Son of man, and drink his blood, ye have no life in you. Whoso eateth my flesh, and drinketh my blood, hath eternal life; and I

will raise him up at the last day. For my flesh is meat indeed, and my blood is drink indeed. He that eateth my flesh, and drinketh my blood, dwelleth in me, and I in him. As the living Father hath sent me, and I live by the Father: so he that eateth me, even he shall live by me. This is that bread which came down from heaven: not as your fathers did eat manna, and are dead: he that eateth of this bread shall live for ever. (vv. 53–58)

When we compare John's account of this story involving bread and water with a similar account with Moses in Exodus 14–17, we experience great peace. With Moses, the crossing of the water at the Red Sea comes first, and then the people receive bread and water in the wilderness. They pass through the judgment waters first and then are given bread in the wilderness. With Jesus the bread in the wilderness comes first, then the crossing of the water at the Sea of Galilee. The disciples eat the bread in the wilderness, and then they pass through the judgment waters. What accounts for the difference in order? It is because of the new covenant. With Moses, the children of God were brought through the waters of judgment, and then they were fed. With Jesus, we are fed and then brought through the waters of judgment. The point is this: the food with which Jesus feeds you is the very food that carries you through the waters of judgment. He feeds you with the true Bread from heaven. He feeds you with Himself. He feeds you with Himself because it is only in Him that you are taken safely through the waters, the storms, and even through the judgment to the new heavens and the new earth.

John will draw upon these same themes in Revelation 15:1–4 to give peace to the children of God. There John writes,

> And I saw another sign in heaven, great and marvellous, seven angels having the seven last plagues; for in them is filled up the wrath of God. And I saw as it were a sea of glass mingled with fire: and them that had gotten the victory over the beast, and over his image, and over his mark, and over the number of his name, stand on the sea of glass, having the harps of God. And they sing the song of Moses the servant of God, and the song of the Lamb, saying, Great and marvellous are thy works, Lord God Almighty; just and true are thy ways, thou King of saints. Who shall not fear Thee, O Lord, and glorify thy name? for thou only art holy: for all nations shall come and worship before thee; for Thy judgments are made manifest.

Notice the order here: the final wrath of God is about to be poured out, but before it is, the saints are pictured standing on the sea of glass, singing the song of Moses and the Lamb. In other words, the saints sing the song of triumph *before* God's wrath is poured out. They are safe and secure. The wrath of God does not touch them. In fact, they are standing *on* the sea of glass. So great is their victory in Christ, the waters are calm beneath their feet; it is as though they were standing on solid ground, and they are singing. No storms, darkness, or fear here. Only joy and gladness and peace are here. Such imagery is suggested already in John 6. John uses creation imagery to tell us Jesus will bring us safely through all the storms of life and even the last judgment, to the peace of the new creation.

Not only has Jesus given us His word that He will bring all who believe on Him into the joy and peace of the new creation, He has also given His Spirit to minister in and through that word for our comfort. As Jesus draws near to the day of His death, when He will bear on the cross the judgment for all whom the Father has given to Him, He ministers to His troubled disciples once again. He says, "Let not your heart be troubled; ye believe in God, believe also in me" (John 14:1). He also makes this promise:

> I will pray the Father, and he shall give you another Comforter, that he may abide with you for ever; even the Spirit of truth; whom the world cannot receive, because it seeth him not, neither knoweth him: but ye know him; for he dwelleth with you, and shall be in you. I will not leave you comfortless: I will come to you.... These things I have spoken unto you, being yet present with you. But the Comforter, which is the Holy Ghost, whom the Father will send in my name, he shall teach you all things, and bring all

things to your remembrance, whatsoever I have said unto you. Peace I leave with you, my peace I give unto you: not as the world giveth, give I unto you. Let not your heart be troubled, neither let it be afraid. (vv. 16–18, 25–27)

The Heidelberg Catechism, question 18, reassures us of Christ's presence: "In his human nature Christ is not now on earth, but in his divinity, majesty, grace, and Spirit he is never absent from us."

Whatever storms you may have experienced, whatever darkness surrounds you right now, whatever storms may come, Jesus is with you by His Spirit. The Spirit ministers through the Word to bring you peace in Jesus. He is no less with you in the midst of the storms of life than He was with the disciples in the midst of the storm in John 6. He will not leave you in this darkness; He will not leave you in the deep; He will not leave you in the storm. He will bring you safely through to the joy of eternal day.

There is peace here for believers. No matter how dark the night may seem to you, darkness will give way to light. No matter how deep and tempestuous the waters may be around you, they will be calmed. No matter how fierce the storm may rage about you, the storm is God's storm. Where do you turn when all around you is darkness, when the storms of life encompass you? Where do you find peace in the hardest times of life? Turn to the Word of God. Look to the joy that He will bring in the morning. Find peace in the promise of the new heavens and the new earth, where you will live in the eternal peace of everlasting day.

CONCLUSION

God's ways with us are often in the waters (Ps. 77:19). Those waters may threaten to overcome and consume you. But He is in control. You need not fear the darkness, the waters, or the storm. You need not fear at all. He is with you, and His word to you is this: "I Am! Do not be afraid!" Let your anxious soul hear His word to you: "Be still, and know that I am God" (Ps. 46:10).

As you recognize that the darkness will come, as you believe that Jesus is on your side, as you listen to His Word, as you reflect on His character, and as you look to the joy that comes in the morning, may you have peace, even the peace that passes all understanding, and may it guard your heart and mind in Christ Jesus.

> O God, our help in ages past,
> Our hope for years to come,
> Our shelter from the stormy blast,
> And our eternal home.
>
> Under the shadow of Thy throne,
> Thy saints have dwelt secure;
> Sufficient is Thine arm alone,
> And our defense is sure.

Before the hills in order stood,
Or earth received her frame,
From everlasting Thou art God,
To endless years the same.

A thousand ages in Thy sight
Are like an evening gone,
Short as the watch that ends the night
Before the rising sun.

Time, like an ever-rolling stream,
Bears all its sons away;
They fly forgotten, as a dream
Dies at the opening day.

O God, our help in ages past,
Our hope for years to come,
Be Thou our guard while troubles last,
And our eternal home.[4]

---

4. William Crofts, "O God, Our Help in Ages Past," in *Psalter Hymnal*, #176.